Christmas Jingles and Santa Kringles

LINE ART PATTERN BOOK
by Annie Lang

When the Kringles start ringing the jingle bells, Christmas isn't far behind! There are dozens of mix and Santa and holida bell designs in this whimsical line art pattern book to use on an Holiday surface you can think of. Create anything from wearable iron-ons and greeting cards to window decals, Christmas decorations, classroom painting projects and more.

Simply trace the design and then transfer the image onto your project surface to make outstanding personalized items with professional results every time.

Transferring the linework designs
Trace the design of your choice with pencil and tracing paper.
Place transfer paper under the tracing paper and place onto
your selected surface. Hold in place with tape if necessary.
Retrace over the linework to transfer the design onto the project.
For fabrics, trace the design, flip the pattern over and retrace
the lines using a fabric transfer pen. Follow manufacturer's
direction to iron the design onto your chosen fabric item.

Color or paint these designs with
Craft paints, watercolors, markers, coloring pencils, chalks,
inks, fabric pens, paint pens, or crayons

These designs are great for
Home Dec Items like furniture, cabinets, accent items, walls,
lamps, glassware, kitchen accessories, office and desk items,
bathroom accents, cabinets, patio pots and outdoor items, etc.
Fabric and wearable items like t-shirts, sweatshirts, aprons,
canvas shoes, totes, quilting squares, table linens and napkins,
window and shower curtains, pillows, etc.
Paper Craft Projects like greeting cards, scrap page elements,
tags, labels, stationery items, ornaments, gift bags, etc.

For more ideas and designer tips, please visit my Blog at
http://annielang-anniethingspossible.blogspot.com/
My Pinterest Board at http://www.pinterest.com/anniethings/
or my Facebook Page at
http://www.facebook.com/anniethingspossible

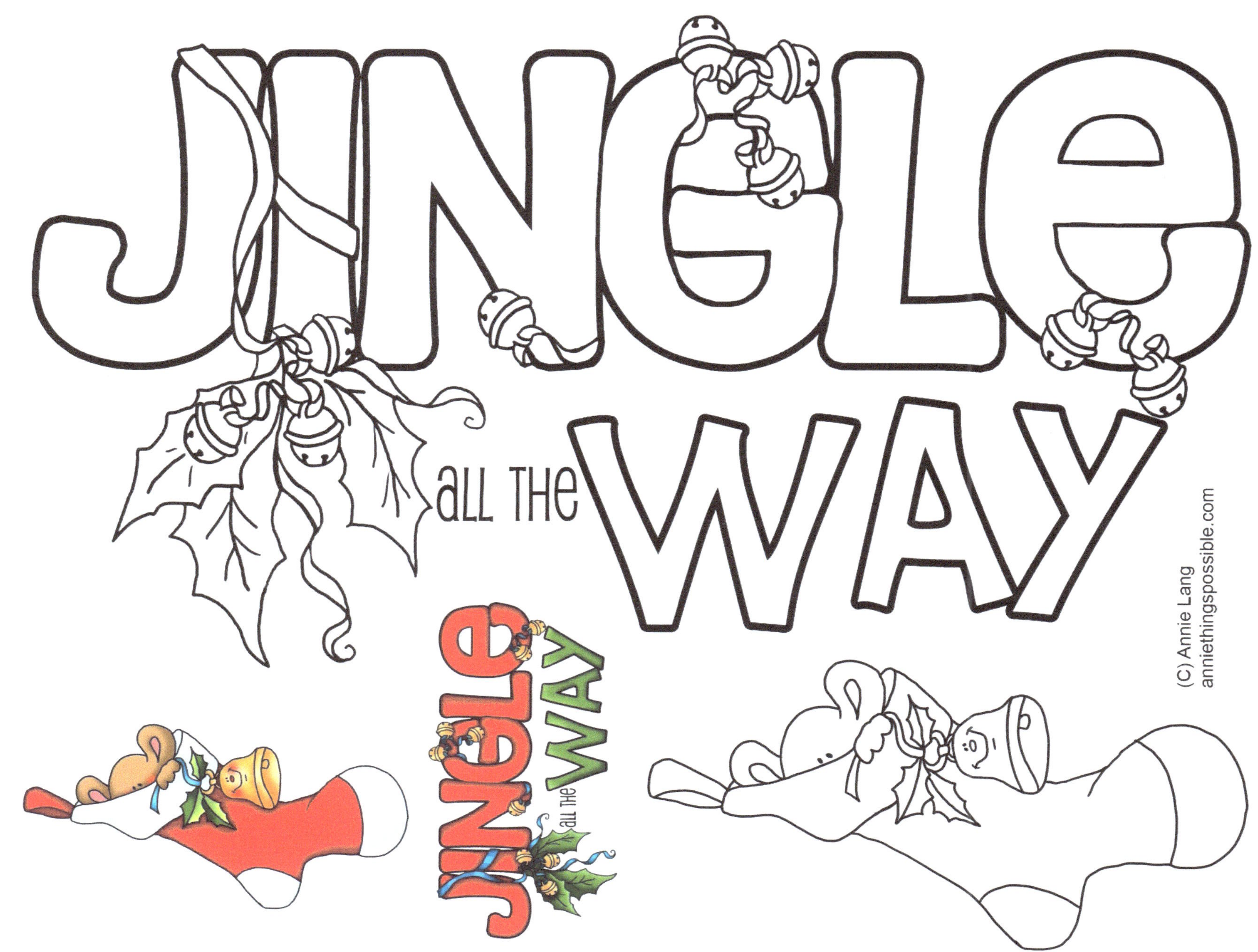
JINGLE all the WAY
JINGLE all the WAY
(C) Annie Lang
anniethingspossible.com

Jingle Mouse

(C) Annie Lang
anniethingspossible.com

Every time a bell rings
an
Angel
gets her
Wings

it's JINGLE time!
it's JINGLE time!
Jingle Puppy
(C) Annie Lang
anniethingspossible.com

(C) Annie Lang
anniethingspossible.com

Jingle On!

Jingle Bear

(C) Annie Lang
anniethingspossible.com

let the
Bells
ring
let the
Bells
ring
(C) Annie Lang
anniethingspossible.com

let the Bells Ring
let the Bells Ring
Jingle Kitty
(C) Annie Lang
anniethingspossible.com

Jingle Santa
(C) Annie Lang
anniethingspossible.com

Jingle Border (C) Annie Lang
anniethingspossible.com

(C) Annie Lang
anniethingspossible.com

(C) Annie Lang
anniethingspossible.com

(C) Annie Lang
anniethingspossible.com

(C) Annie Lang
anniethingspossible.com

No Peeking!

(C) Annie Lang
anniethingspossible.com

(C) Annie Lang
anniethingspossible.com

NORTH POLE
NORTH POLE

Hear the Bells Ring and let Your Heart Sing
Hear the Bells Ring and let Your Heart Sing

Happy
Santa
SMILES

KRINGLES
always
JINGLE

KRINGLES
always
JINGLE

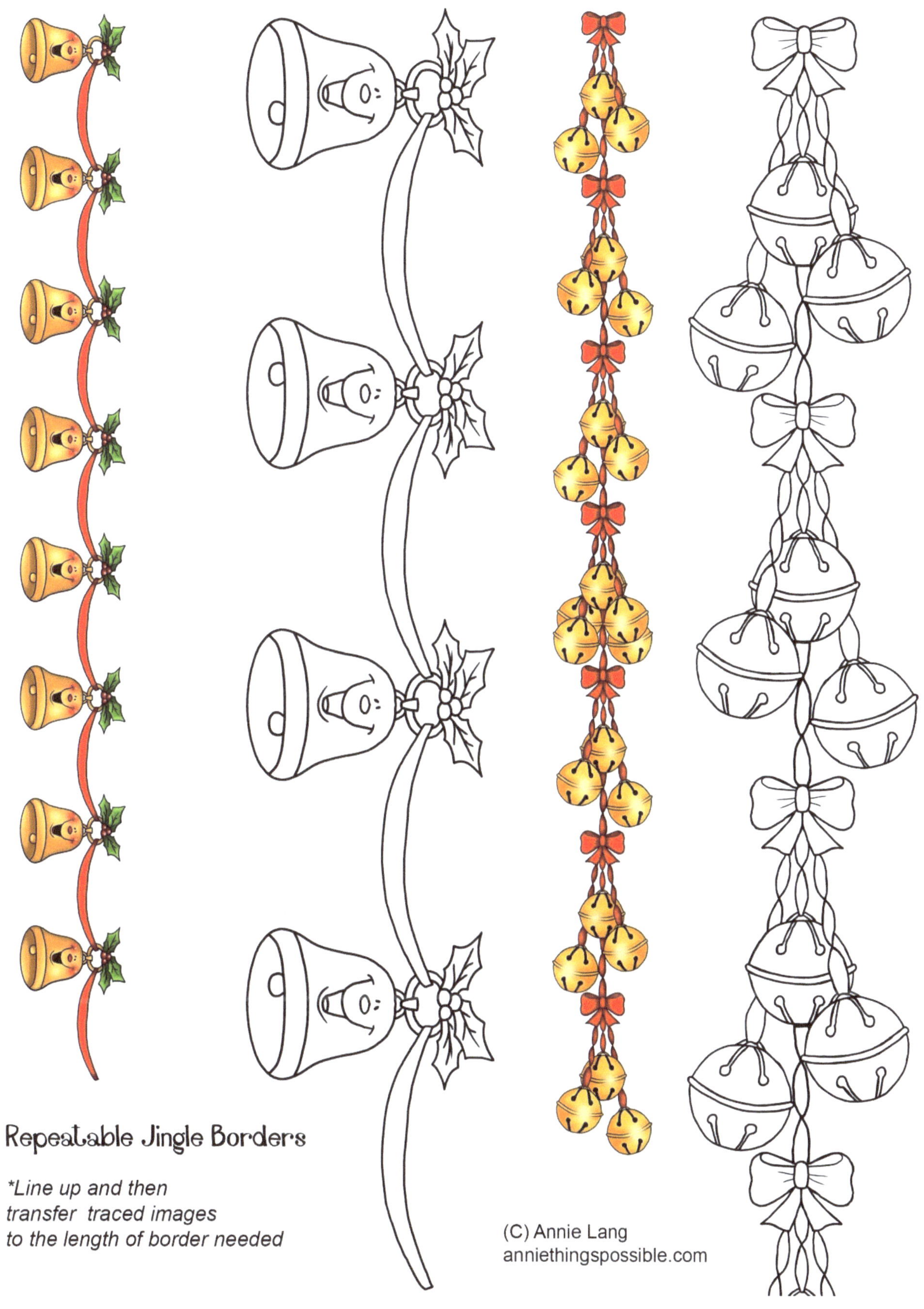

Repeatable Jingle Borders

*Line up and then
transfer traced images
to the length of border needed*

(C) Annie Lang
anniethingspossible.com

(C) Annie Lang
anniethingspossible.com

Thank you for purchasing this publication!

Find dozens of other fun titles on my
Annie Lang's Books website!

I hope you enjoyed this book and
encourage you to leave a review and share your
thoughts for other customers at Amazon.com!

To learn more about the author, get free project
ideas, see video how-to's and more, please visit
Annie Lang's BLOG at
http://annielang-anniethingspossible.blogspot.com/